AD WAMMES

TOCCATINA

MUSIC DEPARTMENT

OXFORD
UNIVERSITY PRESS

to Willem van Twillert

Toccatina

AD WAMMES

I: Octave 4', Rohrflöte 4'
II: Spitzflöte 4'
Ped.: Gedackt 8'
Add I+II coupler if I is unenclosed

Composer's note: The suggested registrations are based upon the possibilities of my Clavia Nord C2 organ. You are welcome to adapt the registrations where necessary.

© Oxford University Press 2021

Printed in Great Britain

OXFORD UNIVERSITY PRESS, MUSIC DEPARTMENT, GREAT CLARENDON STREET, OXFORD OX2 6DP
The Moral Rights of the Composer have been asserted. Photocopying this copyright material is ILLEGAL.

19
I: Gamba 8', Gedackt 8', Rohrflöte 4'
mf
f
(I+II off)
II: Rohrflöte 8' only
mp
+ Subbass 16'
23
27
32

37
41
45
49

53
57
61
65

69
+ Spitzflöte 4'
73
+ Principal 8', Octave 4'
f
mf
77
81

85
89
(I+II on)
93
I: Octave 4', Rohrflöte 4'
II: Spitzflöte 4'
p
Gedackt 8'
p
97

101
mp
105
109
f
113
II: 8's, 4's
mf
I: 8's, 4's
f
16's, 8's + II
mf

118
123
127
f without 16', Reeds
molto f without 16', Reeds
131

135
139
143
147
(II)
(I)
+ Fagot 16'